The Little Book

A Self-Help
Unhelpful Thoughts

Kevin M O'Doherty

First Published in United Kingdom by
Cognitive Therapy books

A CIP catalogue record for this book is available from the British Library.

ISBN No: 978-0-9562641-0-7

About the Author

I began my academic career as a psychology lecturer and moved on to become a health psychologist and cognitive behaviour therapist. At the time of going to print, I am a training manager for a national mental health charity based in Central London, supporting people with enduring mental health issues into education and training. I also have a private CBT practice in Central London, where I continue to see clients on a regular basis.

I decided to write the 'Little Book of Thinking Errors' for very practical reasons. There was no other small, compact and easy to use book that summarised most of the thinking errors that came up in my clinical practice. I wanted to design the book in such a way that it could be used primarily by clients, and people who merely had an interest in the way our thoughts help to shape our feelings. But also, the intention was for the book to be useful to practicing therapists and other health and social care professionals.

On a personal level, I have certainly found that in the process of writing this book, I am much more aware of how important it is to increase awareness of our thinking errors, and of the range of techniques we can use to replace unhelpful thoughts, thus helping to minimise psychological distress.

I very much hope that you will find this book an easy to use, valuable resource. Feedback is always welcomed. Please visit the website below.

Thank you very much for your purchase.

www.cognitivetherapybooks.com

Devoted to the love of my life...Theresa

Whose love, support and encouragement makes all things possible.

I Love You

Contents

10. Over-generalising

11. Over-estimating the dangers

12. Underestimating your ability to cope

13. Minimising or filtering out the positives

14. Magical thinking

15. Placing a Value on yourself as a whole person on the basis of one event

16. Magnifying

17. Jumping to conclusions

18. Assuming there is only one valid view

19. Assuming your view will never change

Foreward

Have you ever found yourself feeling sad about what happened yesterday? Or worrying about what may happen tomorrow? Do you sometimes notice a whole range of disturbing thoughts going round and around in your mind? It was the psychiatrist Aaron Beck in the 1960's who first coined the term 'thinking errors' to describe some of the mistakes we can sometimes make in our thinking, which can play a part in emotional distress. Beck found a close relationship between these thinking errors and depression. Since then, a great deal of research has taken place, confirming the link between the way we think and how we feel.

For Cognitive Behaviour Therapists, helping you to review and amend unhelpful thinking is viewed as being of central importance in the alleviation of emotional distress. Thus, when you begin to work with a CBT therapist, they will help you to develop a deeper understanding of your thought processes, with a view to replacing the unhelpful thoughts, with more constructive and realistic views, that are more conducive to psychological health and wellbeing.

This book lists and describes many of the thinking errors that can play a part in psychological distress and unhappiness. Each thinking error is described using fictitious examples and lots of useful suggestions for challenging the thinking errors are outlined.

Who is this Book Suitable For?

- The Little Book of Thinking Errors is primarily suitable for anyone who is interested in better understanding the link between what they think and how they feel. No prior knowledge of psychology or Cognitive Behaviour Therapy is assumed, or needed.

- People undergoing Cognitive Behaviour Therapy, or any other form of counselling or psychotherapy will find this book a very useful resource.

- CBT Therapists in training will find this book a very useful learning tool to help them identify and remember the many thinking errors there are.

- Practicing CBT Therapists can use the book (and hopefully recommend it to their clients!) in their therapeutic work as a clinical aid/adjunct.

- The book will prove especially valuable in group CBT Therapy.

- Finally, this book will prove to be a very valuable resource for other Health, Welfare, and Social Care professionals, who engage in one to one work with clients.

How To Use this Book

The main aim of this book is to raise awareness of the thinking errors that can play a part in emotional distress and unhappiness. This raising of awareness is in itself, therapeutic, and is the first step towards taking control of the thoughts that can lead to unhappiness, and replacing them with more useful, realistic and constructive alternatives. If you are undergoing CBT therapy, your therapist will guide and support you in the best use of this book. If you are not undergoing CBT therapy, and are using the book independently, here are some tips:

1. Become familiar with each of the thinking errors by regular reading and revising this book. It was created as a

pocket sized book, so that you can carry it around and refer to it on a regular basis.

2. When you become familiar with the thinking errors, begin to keep track of your thoughts and feelings using an ABC form (see appendix 1a at the back of this book for an example). Perhaps to begin with, just record one or two thoughts per day, that go through your mind during a period of worry, anxiety or distress etc.

3. At the end of each day, have a look at some of your recorded thoughts, and see if you can spot one or two of the thinking errors outlined in this book. Perhaps discuss this with a trusted friend or family member.

Ask yourself:

▰ Is this thought helpful to me?

- Is this way of viewing the situation helping me to get what I want?

- Where is the evidence that this thought is true?

- Which thinking error am I making?

- What is the effect of thinking in this way?

- What are the costs and benefits of viewing the situation in this way?

- Am I being helpful, supportive and compassionate towards myself?

- How would a person (whose opinion I respect and value) view this situation?

4. Now try to find more realistic, helpful and compassionate alternatives to the problematic thoughts. Make a note of the

alternative thoughts (see appendix 1b at the back of this book) Again, some people find it useful to enlist the help of a trusted friend or family member with this.

By doing this on a regular basis, you will become much more aware of the thoughts that create problematic feelings for you. The process of reviewing unhelpful thoughts and replacing them with more helpful alternatives will become a very useful habit. With regular repeated practice, you will begin to find that as soon as an unhelpful thought or view comes into your mind, you are able to recognise it and change it, before it begins to cause a problem.

Remember not to become overly concerned if you find yourself using several or more of the thinking errors, it is completely normal. The key thing is that you are raising your awareness, with a view to reviewing and replacing unhelpful ways of thinking in a gradual way. Be supportive and compassionate towards yourself as you go through this exciting process of change.

As you begin to evaluate and review your thinking habits, a whole new world of possibilities will begin to open up for you. You will begin to notice that your feelings begin to shift, in line with the new view you begin to take of the world, yourself and the future.

The possibilities for change and adventure are endless, and you have taken the first step in that journey. Bon Voyage!

Note

If you are anything like the author, you will probably find that you make a number of the thinking errors listed in this book! This is completely normal. The book is designed to help you become more aware of these thinking errors and the effects they can have on your feelings. Secondly, the book is designed to help you begin to work on these errors, with the aim of replacing unhelpful thoughts with more realistic, supportive and compassionate ways of thinking.

Please note that the people referred to in this book are purely fictitious. Any similarities to people living or dead, is purely coincidental.

1. Am I Predicting the Future Negatively?

How many times have you caught yourself thinking, or saying things like; "I know I won't get that job." "The date I have on Tuesday will be a disaster." "It is bound to rain on my birthday"? Put your crystal ball away! Contrary to popular belief, it is not, and never has been possible to predict the future (negatively or otherwise)

Whenever Ian began to form a relationship with a potential partner, he would begin to predict the future negatively, thinking to himself, 'This is bound to fail.', 'She will meet somebody else who is more interesting.', 'My relationships will never work out.' You can imagine the barriers that this negative predicting often put between Ian and a successful relationship. Over time, Ian began to replace these negative predictions with more helpful and realistic views, such as 'Nobody can predict the future.', 'I will make the most of the relationship however long it lasts.' and 'It is better to live and play with the present than try to predict the future.'

We can plan and prepare for the future certainly, but when we predict the future negatively, we begin to create a range of negative emotions such as anxiety, worry and sadness. Sometimes there are situations that we can be aware of, such as a job interview, or a meeting with the bank manager perhaps. Plan for it, prepare for it, do your homework, then deal with it as it happens...Don't try to predict the outcome!

2. Am I Trying to Mind-Read?

Pop psychology programmes and magazines would sometimes have us believe that telepathy works...It doesn't! The ability to read people's minds has been tested time and time again under scientific conditions, and has never been proven. We can sometimes guess what another person might be thinking about if we observe their body language etc., but that's all it is, a guess, or a hunch and will probably be inaccurate.

Jane was very upset, after she waved at her friend Mary on the way to work, but Mary didn't respond. Jane thought; "She doesn't like me; she thinks I am stupid; she has taken offence at something I must have done.etc, etc. Jane ruminated about the reasons for Mary not waving or saying hello to her, and became more and more distressed. Finally she phoned

Mary and asked if everything was ok. It turned out that Mary had broken up with her partner and was very sad and deep in thought that morning.

Remember to check your thoughts for the evidence to support them; don't accept your guess or hunch as factual. Think of it as one possible interpretation of the situation. Remember there are many possible alternatives.

In mindreading situations, ask yourself:

1. Where is the evidence that X is thinking A, B, and C

2. Just because I assume something, does that mean I am right?

3. How can I know what other people are thinking unless I ask them?

3. Am I Catastrophising?

Sometimes referred to as 'making a mountain out of a mole hill' catastrophising involves over-estimating the negative impact of a situation, perhaps thinking of, or referring to it, as 'absolutely dreadful, terrible or awful'

James was in the university library when he dropped a pile of books on the floor in the quiet reading room. After picking the books up and laying them on a nearby table, he quickly left the library and made his way home. On the way home he imagined all the people in the library laughing at him, and perhaps thinking that he was so very clumsy and annoying. This is a prime example of 'catastrophising'. There was no evidence that people in the Library had laughed at James, the reading room remained silent after he had dropped the pile of books.

There was also no evidence that people thought he was clumsy and annoying; he was not able to read their minds and know this information.

When you find yourself catastrophising, remember to take a few minutes to look for the hard evidence of how bad a situation seems to be. Ask yourself:

1. Is this really as bad as I imagine it to be?

2. What can I do to help or change the situation?

3. How is thinking about the situation in this way making me feel?

4. Am I being helpful, supportive and compassionate towards myself?

5. Am I over-estimating the importance of this event/situation?

The answer to catastrophising is to de-catastrophise!

4. Am I Personalising?

During times of stress or worry, we can sometimes take somebody else's comments or behaviour personally, when in fact it has very little to do with us.

Jack's boss at work was very quiet one morning; he appeared to be grumpy and self absorbed. Jack took this personally, and thought that he must have somehow offended or upset his boss. He began to think that, by his actions, he had ruined the very constructive relationship he had developed with his boss. Jack began to feel quite anxious and worried about the situation, affecting his ability to concentrate on the work. At the end of the day, Jack's boss called him into the office for a 'chat'. He explained that he was worried about a very large order he had received from a customer, and whether or not the company would be able to meet the deadline. Jack was relieved that the behaviour of his boss earlier in the day was nothing to do with him. It was now clear that his boss had been worried about something totally unrelated.

If you find yourself taking somebody's comments or behaviour personally, stop and ask yourself:

1. Where is the evidence that this is anything to do with me?

2. What is an alternative explanation for this person's comment or behaviour?

3. How do I feel when I imagine that someone else's behaviour means something about me personally?

From time to time, there are instances where another person may say or do something on purpose to upset or offend us. Remember, this says a lot more about them, than it does about you! If there is very clear evidence that another person has deliberately said or done something to upset you, be assertive but diplomatic. Explain to them how you feel, and explain to them how you expect to be treated in future.

5. Am I Demanding Perfection of Myself or Others?

Remember that, like every other person in the world, you are a fallible, imperfect human being prone to making the occasional mistake. If you or I live to be 130 we will never be perfect, such is our plight as human beings. We will sometimes fall short of the mark, in a variety of ways, and so will the people around us, whether they admit it or not. If you tell yourself that you (or others) should be perfect, you will be sadly disappointed, time and again. It's fine to strive for perfection, as long as you realise that you will never attain it! Whatever you or I do in life, it will never be perfect; it can always be improved upon. If we demand perfection, we will very often beat ourselves up when we don't attain it, leading to a sense of unhappiness, stress and anxiety.

Try to assure yourself that you have done your best, given the knowledge, skills, experience, support and resources that you have. Think about some of the influential people in your life and ask yourself:

1. How often do they make mistakes?

2. How often do they fall short of the mark?

3. Ask them if there are any aspects of their life that they would like to improve. (If they are honest, they will probably tell you about a whole list of things they would like to improve on.)

Remember the proverb: "The person who didn't make mistakes, didn't do anything."

6. Am I Demanding Certainty?

The world is characterised by a certain degree of uncertainty! We can never really know for sure what's around the next corner, or what may happen tomorrow. People change, the world changes, stock markets rise and fall, adversity can seem to strike at the most inopportune moment. Demanding certainty in the world is certain to lead to disappointment at some point when the world falls short of our demands.

Dave set off for work at the normal time of 08.15, arriving at 08.55. He made coffee and began reading his to-do list for the day. He was called to the manager's office, and by 09.45, was informed that the bank he had been employed by for fifteen years, had to make him and many of his colleagues redundant. Dave had, for many years felt comfortable in his job and was sure he would be working for the same company until he retired at the age of 65. The news of his imminent departure obviously came as a big shock for him initially. However, upon reflection, his experience reminded him that nothing is certain in life, except a degree of uncertainty. Dave began to view life as an adventure, with lots of interesting and unexpected twists and turns.

Dave decided to train for a new career after taking some time out of the 9-5 routine. After a twelve month break to travel across America, Dave began his new training as a Cognitive Behaviour Therapist!

We develop many of our greatest coping skills and strategies, by experiencing uncertainty, and dealing with the unexpected. By taking uncertainty in our step, and developing our coping resources for dealing with the unexpected, we strengthen our resilience, fortitude and individuality. Begin to view uncertainty as an opportunity to learn, grow, change and develop.

Accept the world (and all of the people in it) as being, to an extent, unpredictable.

7. Am I Demanding Justice?

We all want to live in a just world, where we feel we are treated equally and fairly all of the time. From our childhood days, we will have developed a sense of right and wrong, of fairness and injustice. There may be occasions, however, when the world seems to fall short of our desires for fairness and justice. On such occasions, we do well to remember that justice needs to be a preference, rather than a demand. A preference about the way you would like the world to be, rather than demanding it be a certain way. Try to think more flexibly about the world and the way that it sometimes works. Become more accepting of the fact that the world is to a certain extent unpredictable. Try to change the things you can, whilst accepting the things that can't be changed.

8. Am I Thinking in Black and White?

Black and white thinking is thinking in extreme ways, which understandably leads to extreme emotions. I'm either successful or a total loser, either they love me or they hate me, either I am rich or I am poor, the essay I did for the University course is either perfect or complete rubbish, etc, etc. Black and white thinking tends to be harsh and unrealistic; things in life are very rarely as clear cut as we imagine them to be. The world is full of grey areas.

Greg was trying to give up smoking, and had been cigarette-free for several weeks. One evening he gave into temptation and had a cigarette from a friend. He said to himself afterwards: "I've totally blown it; the past 6 weeks have been a total waste of time; I'm destined to smoke for the rest of my life, and I've got absolutely no will power". Thinking in this way made Greg feel very low and fatalistic.

If you find yourself thinking in black and white terms, try this exercise: Take a sheet of paper and write the sentence across the top of the page, that seems to be an example of black and white thinking (For example: My essay is complete rubbish.) Now draw a line across the middle of the page. At the left end of the line write: 'My essay is complete rubbish.' Now at the right end of the line write: 'My essay is the best ever.' Now divide the line into another four points. For each point along the line write a comment, ranging from the best ever to complete rubbish. For example, the next point to 'best ever' could be: 'a very good essay that is sure to get a decent grade' the next point might be: 'an average essay that will pass the grade' next to that might be 'I could add to this essay and improve it' and so on. Now have a think about these comments, ranging from one end of the spectrum to the other...Which one is correct? Can you see that it is a matter of opinion? Whether or not people might view this book as excellent or complete rubbish depends on personal opinion. The book is most likely to be very interesting, helpful and informative to some people, in some parts, some of the time. But then, that is my biased opinion of course!

Remember to be realistic and flexible, remind yourself that life is very rarely clear cut, allow yourself to make mistakes, to perform at less than your very best once in a while.

9. Am I Using Should, Must and Have To?

Ultimatums are ultimately unhelpful! Making demands of yourself or others can lead to worry and anxiety. Instead of using statements such as *I should*, *I must*, *I have to,* etc, try to use:

I aim to...

I prefer to...

I hope to...

I choose to...

I will...

I shall endeavour to...

In this way we turn our demands and ultimatums into preferences, thereby helping to alleviate worry and anxiety. When we think in terms of should, must and have to, we imply that there is a big book of standards somewhere, which lays down all the rules regarding what should and should not be the case. This book, sadly, does not exist.

When you find yourself talking or thinking in ultimatum terms, ask yourself:

1. Why 'should' x be the case?

2. What is the effect of viewing things in this way?

3. How might I feel differently if I began thinking in terms of preferences instead of ultimatums?

Try this exercise: Take a sheet of paper and draw a line down the middle of the page. Label the left hand column 'Must and Should' and the right hand column 'Aims and Preferences'. Now in the left hand column, write down all of the 'Should' and 'Must' statements that come to mind. Now write beside those statements in the right hand column the equivalent preference statements. For example 'I should wash the car.' becomes I aim to wash the car.' and I should not feel anxious.' becomes 'I would prefer not to be anxious'. 'I have to complete my to-do list at work today.' becomes: 'I will endeavour to complete the items on my to-do list.'

Notice how, just by changing a few simple words and thoughts, we can help bring about a whole new way of feeling about a situation.

10. Am I Over-generalising?

All men are bad, relationships never work out, people are not nice, work is always boring, I am never lucky, etc. Does any of this sound familiar? Over-generalising is where we take our experiences from one or two isolated events and make broad, general assumptions about groups of people or future experiences. It is easy to see the distress and unhappiness that can be caused by over-generalising. Be aware of when you use words like never, always, everybody...you could be over-generalising.

Whilst in therapy, Jenny was helped to see that the two unsuccessful relationships she had experienced recently, with men who did not value and respect her, said something about those two individual men. She began to realise that her recent experiences said nothing about men in general because men are all individuals with a whole range of characteristics. We all have some characteristics that are very likeable (even loveable hopefully!) then there will be aspects of our persona or behaviour that others may find annoying.

For Jenny then: 'All men are bad.' became: 'Men are all individuals.' and 'Some men will have characteristics that I am not attracted to.' Jenny began to feel more empowered in her approach to relationships and realised that she has choice with whom she entered a relationship.

11. Am I Over-estimating the Dangers?

This thinking error can be quite common for people who have anxiety disorders or phobias. For somebody who is very fearful of using trains for example, they may think: 'The train is bound to crash. I am totally trapped. I am going to suffocate. Something dreadful is going to happen' It is perhaps easy to see the distress that over-estimating dangers can cause.

John sometimes over-estimated the dangers of travelling on the London Underground. He often imagined the train crashing or getting stuck in the tunnel. This over-estimating of the dangers caused John a great deal of anxiety. He decided to look at the research about accidents on the London Underground, and was surprised to find that statistically, it was actually one of the very safest ways to travel through the busy capital. He decided to put his fears to the test and begin travelling every day on the London Underground, starting with one station, then a second station then third, fourth, and fifth, etc. After several days be began to notice his levels of anxiety whilst on the train began to subside. His estimation of the dangers involved in travelling on the Underground was also lowered.

If you find yourself over-estimating dangers of an every-day situation, ask yourself:

1. Is this really as dangerous as I imagine it to be?

2. Where is the evidence that this situation is dangerous?

3. What is the likelihood of a dangerous outcome?

4. Have I dealt with this situation in the past?

5. What is the worst thing that could happen?

There are of course some situations that may have an element of risk involved, and we would do well to take the necessary precautions in order to minimise the risks as far as possible.

12. Am I Underestimating my Ability to Cope?

3. What coping strategies have I used in the past that may be of use to me in this situation?

Remember to tell yourself you have coped, you can cope and that you will continue to cope in the future.

13. Am I Minimising, or Filtering out the Positives?

This happens when we filter out the positive aspects of a situation and focus on the negatives. It can be likened to throwing out the baby with the bathwater! If, for example, we experience several challenging situations during the day, we may be tempted to say or think: 'the whole day has been a complete disaster' or 'everything has gone wrong today. The day has been awful.' If we look back at such a day, we will most likely find that there were a number of things that actually went well, or according to plan. When we minimise or filter out the positives, we only focus on what the negatives might have been and feel miserable or depressed as a result. Try, therefore, to take a balanced view of each day.

At the end of a day that has involved a number of challenges for you; take a sheet of paper and divide it into two columns. Label the left column 'What went well today' and the right hand column: 'What did not go very well'. Then list all the things that went well, and perhaps not so well.

This exercise will remind you that each day is made up of a number of situations, some seeming to go better than others. This exercise also helps us to take a more balanced view of the day, the meeting, the interview, the date or whatever the situation might be.

14. Am I Using Magical Thinking?

This thinking error occurs when we assume that our thoughts can impact on the physical world around us. More specifically when we use magical thinking, we imagine that our thoughts can actually cause or prevent something from happening.

Lionel would sometimes have a passing thought in his mind that a member of his family had been involved in a road traffic accident. He would immediately try to eliminate this thought from his mind, and would become very anxious each time the thought returned. Lionel thought that he might be responsible were such an accident to happen, if he allowed himself to think about it for any length of time. He became increasingly anxious at the nature of these thoughts, and his underlying belief was that just having the thought could be enough to bring about the feared event.

Remember, we cannot bring about changes in the physical world around us, by the power of thought. You can put this to the test by thinking for the next 30 minutes that the picture you have hanging on the wall will fall off. Try this experiment a number of times throughout the day and see what happens.

(The author accepts no responsibility for any possible damage to your property!)

Alternatively, think for the next 30 minutes that you are going to have a large win on the lottery tomorrow. Please let the author know if this prediction comes to fruition!

15. Am I Placing a Value on Myself as a Whole Person on the Basis of One Event?

James was a therapist. He once in a while had to cancel and then re-schedule a meeting with a client, due to unforeseen events. On one such occasion, he labelled himself as a 'bad' therapist, perhaps one that was 'unprofessional' and 'unreliable'. This line of thinking helped to produce a feeling of inferiority and anxiety. When James began to have a closer look at the situation he realised he was making once of the classic thinking errors (placing a value on himself as a whole person on the basis of one or two events)

You are a complex, multi-faceted human being with a vast range of knowledge, experience, qualities, thoughts, memories, opinions, attitudes, beliefs and feelings. It is not realistic to place a simplistic value on yourself as X, Y or Z on the basis of a single event, or even a whole string of events. When you find yourself making this error, ask the questions:

1. Am I being fair and supportive to myself here?

2. How can I justify passing judgement on myself on the basis of one or two events?

3. Does this way of thinking, help me to get what I want, and feel how I want to feel?

4. Would somebody else (whose opinion I value and trust) place such a value on me, or themselves in this way?

5. Is it helpful and realistic to think that my value as a person is dependent on what I do, or fail to do?

16. Am I Magnifying?

Things are rarely as bad as we imagine they are. When we feel anxious, worried or stressed, we can sometimes blow things out of proportion or 'magnify' Visualise yourself using a gigantic magnifying glass to look at a negative situation, which then seems five times bigger than it actually is. That's exactly what we do when we magnify.

Charlie didn't get the grades he had hoped for in his exams. He immediately thought to himself; 'I have failed miserably, I will never get into the university of my choice, my career plans are ruined, my world is at an end.' Clearly, he was magnifying the implications of this situation.

Think about an issue that causes you to worry or feel anxious and ask yourself:

1. Is it really as bad as I imagine it to be?

2. How many times in the past have my worries turned out to be untrue or exaggerated?

3. What is the effect of magnifying this problem?

4. What is a more realistic way of looking at this issue?

5. On the grand scheme of things, how relevant is this?

6. How much will this matter to me next month? Next year? In five years time?

Remember: we only need to use a magnifying glass when we can't see clearly!

17. Am I Jumping to Conclusions?

This one is similar to predicting the future. 'Jumping to Conclusions' involves making assumptions without looking at all of the evidence. If this is an error that you find yourself making from time to time, try to brush up on your scientific skills and look for the hard evidence before making those assumptions. When scientists develop a theory and a hypothesis to explain an event, they start off by testing the idea scientifically. Typically they set up an experiment, measure the outcome, analyse the results very closely, and then they write their conclusions, etc. Try adopting a more scientific view in relation to thoughts that create unhappiness or distress for you, stand back omit and evaluate the evidence both for and against the troubling thought.

Draw a line down the centre of a sheet of paper, label the left hand column 'Evidence for' and the right hand column 'Evidence against'. At the top centre of the page, write the thought or assumption that you find troubling. Take time to list as much evidence as you can for and against the assumption. You will often find very little evidence in support of the unhelpful thought or assumption. If there seems to be ample evidence to support the troubling thought, then it's time to problem solve; make a list of all the things you can do to help solve the problem, who can you call on for help, advice and support?

Remember a problem shared is a problem halved, share it with three people and the problem is quartered!

18. Am I Assuming there is Only One Valid View?

There is always a multitude of possible ways to look at, or view, a given situation. To put this to the test, ask six people about their view of a topic in the news at the moment, you will very likely find six different views.

John, a newly qualified teacher, was unavoidably late for class one morning. Whilst walking along the corridor to his first lesson of the day, he imagined all of the students in the class having negative views about his lateness. Perhaps they would all think he was unprofessional, disorganised, a bad teacher who should be setting a good example? He surprised the students by giving them all a slip of paper to write down their thoughts and opinions about the teacher being late for his class. To allay their fears, he asked them not to write their name on the slip of paper. On reading the slips, John found that student A thought he was unprofessional, student B thought it was cool that he was a 'real' person who was late once in a while, student C thought that it was 'Totally ok' for a teacher to be late, student D had worried that John was late because of an accident, student E was angry that they may have to be taught by a supply teacher who he didn't know, student F thought it was quite amusing that the teacher was late for class.

Take a sheet of paper and write at the top, an issue that is in the news at the moment. Now write 10 different ways of viewing the issue. You will find that different views will often elicit different emotions such as anger, frustration, joy, amusement, horror, pleasure and excitement.

Remind yourself regularly that there is a whole multitude of different ways to view any given situation. Whichever view is chosen will be a matter of opinion.

19. Am I Assuming my View Will Never Change?

The way we think about a given situation is in constant flux; we review, change and develop our views, moment by moment. Our views continue to change throughout our life in the light of new experiences, information and relationships with other people. Our thoughts about a situation in the morning will have changed or developed by the afternoon. Our thoughts even change and develop minute by minute, as we analyse, examine, seek the advice or opinion of others, and consider all of the evidence, etc.

It is important from time to time to take a step back from our view of a situation, and consider how it has changed and developed over time. As you begin to take control of your thinking, by raising awareness of thinking errors and by using the exercises in this book, you will notice that your views on a whole range of issues will begin to change.

Try not to worry too much about thoughts and ideas that come into your mind by reminding yourself that they are likely to be temporary.

Imagine yourself to be standing on the platform at a train station when a train that is going to an unpopular destination arrives. You can choose to board the train and go to the place that is not nice, or you can simply choose to remain on the platform and watch the train pass right through the station.

Use this analogy when unpleasant thoughts come into your mind...you can choose to board the train of thought, or just allow it to pass by in its own time.

20. Am I Assuming that Nobody can help?

In the United Kingdom, the United States and many other countries in the world, there is a help/advice line or support group for almost every situation or eventuality one can think of. Whatever the situation you are experiencing, you are not alone, many other people will have gone through, or are going through the exact same situation. Do some research and link up with a group or organisation that can provide help, advice and support for the problem you are experiencing. If you have access to the internet, try typing into a search engine: 'help and support for' then type in the problem or difficulty you are facing. You will find a great deal of information on the subject, together with groups and organisations that can help, advise and support you.

Remember that friends, family and neighbours can also be a very valuable source of support with difficulties and challenges. We may sometimes think that we wouldn't like to burden our friends or family with a worry or difficulty we have. Often, friends and loved ones will feel complimented by the fact that you trust and value them enough to seek their help and advice.

If there appears to be no help, advice or support groups in your local area for the issue you are experiencing, perhaps you could look into setting one up?

There are a range of advice and support organisations listed at the end of this book, together with a number of websites that provide CBT over the internet.

21. Am I Assuming I can (or should) change other people's behaviour?

Remember, you can never change other people's behaviour; that is their right and responsibility to do so, if and when they choose to. You can only change the way that you respond to their behaviour.

Jack had a friend Jim who would not return his telephone calls, and who was not very supportive when his help was needed. Jack became very angry and distressed when he thought, 'Jim is incredibly selfish, he should phone me every other day, he should visit me and see how I am getting on, why isn't he more helpful, supportive?' Jack began to realise that this situation had been happening on a regular basis, despite the fact that he had repeatedly pointed out to Jim the error of his ways. Jack began to feel more at ease when he realised that Jim was Jim, and that only he could change his own behaviour. Jack realised also that Jim was not the kind of friend he would like in his life any longer, and decided to end the friendship.

The experience had taught Jack a very valuable lesson: we can change our own behaviour, we can change the way we respond to other people's behaviour, but we can't change other people's behaviour.

22. Am I Using 'What-if's'?

What if I am made redundant? What if I develop heart disease? What if my car gets stolen during the night? What if I leave my wallet on the bus? What if? What if? What if?...The list can sometimes seem to be endless. Our mind can sometimes go round and around in circles, worrying about all the possible problems that may arise. Try to be aware of when you are worrying about 'what if' and perhaps make a list of all the 'what if' sentences you have been worrying about. Now take away the 'what' from the beginning of the sentence and add 'what then' at the end. Now, for each possible problem, make a list of all the things you could do, if the imagined problem actually happened. So for example;

What if I am made redundant? Becomes:

If I am made redundant...**What then**?

Now make a list of all the things you could possibly do if the 'what if' scenario actually happens.

So if Mr X is made redundant from his job, he can have a break, seek advice and support from the careers or employment service, brush up his CV, develop an action plan, retrain, start applying for new jobs, phone friends to ask about any opportunities they are aware of, register with several employment agencies, offer his services to a volunteer organisation.

Thoughts and sentences that begin with 'what if' tend to disempower us and help to create a great deal of worry and anxiety. By turning the thought around, and focusing on the things you could do, in the given situation, you become more empowered, and are more aware of your options and opportunities, making you less likely to worry and ruminate.

Once we begin to replace 'what if' thoughts with 'what then' we become empowered and this opens up a whole range of possibilities for dealing with the eventuality (if it ever happens).

Ask yourself: what if the sun doesn't rise tomorrow morning?

23. Am I Comparing Myself Negatively to Others?

John is much better than me at designing websites, Charlie is more handsome than I am, Mary earns far more money than I do, William lives in a bigger house, etc. etc. Perhaps all of us can think of other people who seem to be better at A, B or C, or have more of X, Y or Z...So what! We all have a range of qualities, skills, assets, good points, experiences etc, that are part and parcel of who we are. We may seem to be ahead of people in some departments and a little behind in others, we can't be good at everything. Remember the point made earlier, none of us will ever be perfect.

Jane was a college lecturer on her way to work when her car came to a halt with a flat tyre. She had never experienced this before, and didn't know what to do. When a helpful passer by stopped and helped her by changing her wheel for the one in the boot, she was very grateful. On the way to work afterwards, however, she began to be self critical. She thought: 'He made it look so easy. He knows all about motor mechanics. I am supposed to be intelligent, but I couldn't even change a flat tyre.' Jane was comparing herself negatively to the passer by who was obviously experienced in car maintenance (or at least in changing wheels!). She had overlooked the need to give herself credit for all the skills and abilities that she has. She could have asked herself 'I wonder if that passer-by could prepare seven lectures per week and present to over a hundred students at a time?

Stop making unfair comparisons, you will be ahead in some areas and perhaps appear to be behind in others. Remember, you can't be good at everything, you're not superhuman!

Ask yourself:

1. Am I making fair comparisons?

2. Am I acknowledging all of the excellent qualities that I have?

24. Am I Using Self Put-Downs?

If there is one sure way to create sadness and depression, it is by putting yourself down, or calling yourself negative names. Be careful to avoid treating yourself unfairly in this way.

When he made a mistake, John would say to himself: 'That's just typical of me, I'm so stupid, and I am a real dumbo, stupid, stupid, stupid.' When John began to monitor the number of self put-downs he used during an average day, he was shocked and surprised. He traced the habit back to when he was a child, and he was regularly criticised by his father for making the occasional mistake. John took his father's negative, critical habit on board, and had been putting himself down for most of his adult life.

Be kind and compassionate to yourself. Would you criticise and put down a very good friend for making the occasional mistake? If not, why would you want to treat yourself in that way? Be your own best friend, value and respect yourself, you're worth it!

Make a list of all your qualities, all the things that you are good at, all of your achievements, all of the challenges that you have overcome. Now focus on that list, perhaps stick it on your refrigerator...Pretty impressive isn't it?

25. Am I Using Double Standards?

Tracy and her friend Louise had both been single for several years. Tracy thought that Louise was single because she had not met the right person yet, because she chose and preferred to be independent, and because she was waiting for the right person to come along. When thinking about the reasons why she, herself was single however, Tracy thought it was because she was unattractive, because people found her to be boring. She thought she would probably always be single, and she would be lonely for the rest of her life. Tracy was using 'double standards' i.e. applying one set of standards to other people, but a separate (negative, harsh and unhelpful) set of standards to herself.

Remember, you need to have or develop a flexible, fair and compassionate set of standards, which you apply evenly and fairly to yourself and others.

If your find yourself using double standards, ask yourself:

1. How can this be fair?

2. How does it make me feel to apply a harsher, more rigid set of standards for my own behaviour than to others behaviour?

Remember what's good for the goose is also good for the gander!

26. Am I Using Emotional Reasoning?

This is where we take our feelings as representative of reality, thus; if we feel anxious, we automatically assume that there must be something to be anxious about.

Jan felt very anxious whilst walking home from work one evening, she just 'knew' something terrible was about to happen. The anxious thoughts she was having, lead to anxious feelings, which she interpreted as a sure sign that something bad was about to happen. Again remember to look for the evidence that something bad is about to happen. Your feelings are not factual; they are your interpretation of a situation. Remember that there is a whole range of different ways to interpret a given situation.

Your feelings are a hunch about the external world. Remember hunches can turn out to be incorrect. Try to distance yourself from your feelings, and see them for what they are... feelings. Ask yourself:

1. How often in the past have my feelings turned out to be incorrect?

2. What evidence do I have that my feelings are correct?

27. Am I Fretting Over Questions that Can't be Answered?

1. How many people will buy this book?

2. How many books will I write?

3. How long will I live?

4. Will I develop a serious health problem one day?

5. Is the current recession going to turn into a 'great depression' as some of the newspapers would have me believe?

These are all questions that have no answers, or, at least, they have no answers that are knowable! I will have to wait and see, so it makes no point worrying myself about them. We can perhaps, all think of questions from time to time that help create uncertainty and anxiety, but to which there are no answers. Be aware of situations where you are posing unanswerable questions to yourself that create anxieties or worry. Ask yourself:

1. Is it possible for me to answer this question?

2. Can somebody else answer this question for me?

3. Does this question need to be answered?

4. What is the effect of posing this kind of unanswerable question to myself?

5. Is it better for me to wait and see what the answer will be?

Summary

This book has hopefully given you a very clear introduction to a range of thinking errors, which can lead to unhappiness or emotional distress. In addition, the helpful guidance and tips will enable you to begin the process of replacing unhelpful thoughts with ways of thinking about yourself, the world and the future that are much more aligned with psychological health and wellbeing.

Where to Now?

Like learning any new skill, the process of changing the way we think takes time, patience and practice. Our thinking styles will have developed over many years, and will have been shaped and moulded by a whole range of experiences. Remember to be patient with yourself as you begin to break old thinking habits, learn new skills and move forward in new directions.

Be aware that whenever you are feeling negative emotions such as worry, anxiety or depression, it is time to have a closer look at the thoughts that have been going through your mind. If the thoughts are negative, harsh, self critical, demanding or unfair in any other way, challenge them! Once you get into the habit of catching your thoughts before they begin to take root and cause problems, you will find it much easier to alleviate negative emotions.

Once you replace the unhelpful thoughts with views that are more helpful, realistic and supportive, try writing them in your diary, or on post-it notes that you can place around the house, on the dresser or refrigerator perhaps. The new set of thoughts will take time to become part of your every-day vocabulary. Use whatever techniques you find are helpful, to remind yourself of the more realistic thoughts and beliefs. If you find yourself slipping back into old habits, just review the work that you have done, re-read this book, or re-visit some of the exercises.

Changing the way that you think takes time and practice, but it's not difficult. Remember it's like all the other skills you have mastered in your life, practice makes perfect!

I wish you the very best for the future and would like to take this opportunity to thank you for your purchase. I will be writing more self-help books in the future, aimed at helping you to master the art of using Cognitive Behaviour Therapy techniques for every-day situations. Remember to check out the website below for news and developments, new releases and much more.

Also, if you have any questions or comments; your feedback is very much valued; please do this by logging onto the publisher's website at:

www.cognitivetherapybooks.com

Additional Help and Support

This book is not designed or intended as a diagnostic tool, or a treatment manual for psychological difficulties, rather it is a self help guide to understanding and replacing some of the thinking errors that can play a part in psychological distress.

If you feel that you need professional help with your thoughts or feelings, please consult one of the many organisations offering professional help and support, listed below. The organisations listed are based in the United Kingdom and the United States respectively. If you do not live in one of these countries, please consult your Medical Practitioner or your local advice and information centre, for further help, advice and information.

Help and Support in the UK

Alcoholics Anonymous
PO Box 1, Stonebow House, Stonebow
York, Y01 2NJ. Tel: 01904 644 026

Anxiety UK
Zion Community Resource Centre
339 Stretford Rd, Hulme, Manchester
M15 4ZY. Tel: 0870 7700 456
Web: www.anxietyuk.org.uk

Association of Post-Natal Depression
25 Jerdan Place, Fulham, London,
SW6. Tel: 0207 836 0868

*(BABCP) British Association for
Behavioural and Cognitive
Psychotherapies*, The Globe Centre
PO Box 9, Accrington, BB5 OXB.
Tel: 01254 875 277

Web: www.babcp.org.uk

Depression Alliance   PO Box 1022,
London, SE1 7GR. Tel: 0207 721 7672

Manic Depressive Fellowship
8-10 High Street, Kingston Upon Thames
London, KT1 1EY. Tel: 0208 974 6550

MIND, The National Association for Mental Health, Granta House, 15-19
Broadway, Stratford, London, E15 4BQ.
Tel: 0208 519 2122

Web:www.mind.org.uk

No Panic, 93 Brands Farm Way, Telford,
TF3 2JQ. Tel: 01952 590 005
Web: www.nopanic.org.uk

OCD Action
Aberdeen Centre
22-24 Highbury Grove London, N5 2EA.
Tel: 0808 808 0545
Web: www.ocdaction.org.uk

Help and Support in the United States

American Mental Health Foundation
2 East 86th Street, New York, NY 1008

Anorexia Nervosa and Related Eating Disorders, Inc, PO Box 5102
Eugene, or 97405.
Tel: 541 344 1144
Web: www.anred.com

Anxiety Disorders Association of America 8730 Georgia Avenue, Suite 600, Silver Spring, MD 20910.
Tel: 240 485 1001, Web: www.adaa.org

Association for the Advancement of Behaviour Therapy, 305 Seventh Avenue, New York, NY 1001-6008
Tel: 212 647 1890

Kidscope, Obsessive Compulsive Foundation, PO Box 70, Milford CT 06460-0070

National Alliance for the Mentally Ill, 200 N. Glebe Rd, Suite 1015, Arlington, VA 22203-3754. Tel: 800 950 6264

National Anxiety Foundation, 3135 Custer Drive, Lexington, KY 40517-4001. Tel: 606 272 7166

National Foundation for Depressive Illness, PO Box 2257, New York, NY 10116. Tel: 800 248 4344

National Mental Health Association, 1201 Prince Street, Alexandria, VA 22314-2971. Tel; 703 684 7722

Useful Websites for Online CBT

www.moodgym.com

www.beatingtheblues.co.uk

www.firefighter.com

The Author's Private Practice Website

www.mindhigherheart.com

Further Reading

Padesky, C. A and Greenberger, D. (1995) *Mind Over Mood; Change How You Feel by Changing the Way You Think*. Guildford Press, London.

Fennell, M. (1999) *Overcoming Low Self Esteem; A Self-help guide using Cognitive Behavioural Techniques*. Robinson, London.

Wilson, R. And Branch R. (2006) *Cognitive Behavioural Therapy for Dummies*. John Wiley and Sons, London.

Gilbert, P. Overcoming Depression: A Self-help guide using Cognitive Behavioural Techniques. Robinson, London.

Tricket, S. (1996) Overcoming Anxiety and Depression: Robinson, London

What Happened?	Thoughts/Beliefs	Feelings

Appendix A2: Example ABCD Recording Form

Date:

What Happened?	Thoughts/Beliefs	Feelings	Alternative Thoughts/Beliefs

The End

Л